D0039036

creatures of a day

POEMS

REGINALD GIBBONS

Louisiana State University Press

Baton Rouge

NATIONAL
ENDOWMENT
FOR THE ARTS

This publication is supported in part by an award from the National Endowment for the Arts.

Published by Louisiana State University Press
Copyright © 2008 by Reginald Gibbons
All rights reserved
Manufactured in the United States of America
First printing

Designer: Barbara Neely Bourgoyne
Typeface: Brioso Pro, display; Minion Pro, text
Printer and binder: Thomson-Shore, Inc.

Library of Congress Cataloging-in-Publication Data

Gibbons, Reginald.
  Creatures of a day : poems / Reginald Gibbons.
    p. cm.
  ISBN 978-0-8071-3317-0 (cloth : alk. paper) — ISBN 978-0-8071-3318-7 (pbk. : alk. paper)
  I. Title.
  PS3557.I1392C73 2008
  811'.54—dc22

                                                                    2007034185

The author is grateful to the editors who first published poems now collected in this volume. (Some of them bore different titles and were worded differently.) These poems are "At a twenty-four-hour gas station," "Sometimes there's neither sun nor shadow," and "I had been reading ancient Greeks": *American Poetry Review*; "In cold spring air" and "These sideways leaps, remembering": *DoubleTake / Points of Entry*; "Citizens": *Iowa Review*; "Samaritan": *Nightsun*; "Celebration" and "On sad suburban afternoons of autumn": *Ontario Review*; "An aching young man": *A Public Space*; "In an old cabinet": *Literary Imagination*.

"Confession," "Rich pale pink" (as "Sky"), "Sleepless in the cold dark" (as "Hour"), "The young woman did office work," and "Where moon light angles through" (as "Train Above Pedestrians") first appeared in *Poetry* magazine, copyright © 2003, 2004, and 2006 by the Poetry Foundation, and are reprinted with permission of the editor. "Confession," "Enough," and "My Herakleitos" were included in the chapbook *In the Warhouse,* published by Fractal Edge Press (2004). *Fern-Texts* was first published as a chapbook by Hollyridge Press (2005), and for that, special thanks to Ian Wilson.

The paper in this book meets the guidelines for permanence and durability of the Committee on Production Guidelines for Book Longevity of the Council on Library Resources. ∞

DRIFTWOOD PUBLIC LIBRARY
801 SW HWY 101
LINCOLN CITY, OREGON 97367

Contents

creatures of a day

Ode: Citizens

In the long shadows of the Chicago mountains, I walk past a very old
      woman, she's tiny, pushing down the sidewalk in the other direction
      a grocery-store basket over-filled with her homeless possessions
      without price, maybe she's

She's the same age as Mother, at the very end, she looks very like Mother,
      with the same large, startling, intense and made-up eyes, and she
      stares

And stares at me with autumn clarity, and when I look back at her she is
      still staring, having stopped and half-turned, but I go on—instead
      of responding to her and asking, "Auntie?"

And asking who she is, asking whom she recognizes in me, taking that
      opportunity of a split second to speak to this stranger, but it passes
      before I have let myself feel

Fully the impulse to speak, the need to speak, I move on, the distance

The gap between us is too great and I don't want to turn around and see if
      she is still watching me,

Maybe she is, I feel guilty—her existence is knowable but willfully not
      known by people like me—yet this is not an aunt of whom I never
      knew, nor is it Mother herself as I never knew her,

As I needed to know her, or rather as I needed her to be,

To be knowable to me emotionally,

To be capable of knowing me,

This is an old woman I don't know who could use twenty dollars and a
      different life,

A different history

For herself and for everyone,

And for her realness I await no metaphor (they do come when the arteries of
thought are calmly open),

This is not a moment amazingly full of a conversation that has never before
been spoken, a discovery to overturn everything, finally an exchange
of revelations.

~

From somewhere, a family, a village, a neighborhood, comes

The solitary singer, maybe with a guitar, who pauses with her burdens and
sings, or the wayfaring man with a story that began somewhere else
who stops under a tree and plays a dance on his violin, even if no one
listens or dances,

Dances or even listens, for there is pain and there is hope—some of the pain

Produced impersonally by remote traders in policy, some of the pain produced

By an ever tighter knotting of constraints around our inward leap to escape,
some of the hope

Used against those who hope, postponing their desires and displacing their
attempts to choose onto clothes and stars and which streets to wander.

~

After a waitress brings three plates of hot food from which steam is rising
delicately, a thin woman in a booth behind mine in a diner says to her
two companions, "I only eat dark meat," her voice is apologetic, she
wants to be helped—"Actually, I only eat the wings . . . ," she says,

"Really, I only eat part of the wings," she's about fifty, and the two men sitting
opposite her, each with a glass of beer to wash down the grub, are in
their seventies, and in a softer voice she says to the shorter one, "Can I
call you Uncle Sid?"

And there seems to be a small party in the back room for a new young fire-
man, who will try to save the uncles who have built the diners and
taverns and the aunts who have waited on the customers, and the
customers, too, if they are caught inside the fiercest heat of what is
burning us.

~

Near me in a coffee shop, are two imperfect persons in their forties, perhaps
from the nearby halfway house, the woman is nodding, almost en-
tirely silent, as the man talks and talks in halfway words, a kind of
disabled philosopher giving a disjointed discourse

On beauty, on his fingers, on gaining exactly one pound of body weight last
week, on Israel, but as if the woman weren't there,

Does she even know him?—and she nods to him with her upper body in a
kind of self-restrained homage of rocking, he's her lost brother, she
hopes or fears,

Neither of them has any longer the habit of combing or brushing hair, he
half-rises, he leans across the table and kisses her cheek.

~

Because in some village there will yet be a wedding that lasts three days,

Because sometimes the solitary singer, maybe with a guitar, pauses in her
journey and sings, or the wayfaring man who knows a world some-
where else stops under a tree and plays a melancholy dance on his
violin,

And after picking or threshing all day in Kosovo or Michoacán or Missis-
sippi, singing softly together while riding in a tractor-cart, the har-
vesters go back tired to the small town to get a beer,

And in Illinois on the raw graded earth that will be a road the builders walk
away from the monstrous machines turned off and turn on their own
pickups, their radios shout,

And the late-night workers in Chicago restock the shelves or suit up in their
   clown costumes and begin to fry and sell hamburgers or in their
   pajamas they strain motionlessly over the report that is due, because
   there is resignation yet there can still be a plan.

~

The city's restless movement never ceases in the streets, everyone has things
   to do, and on the same streets the beggars and wanderers and the
   out-of-work and the thinkers and the grieving do almost nothing,
   and in offices people are performing or pretending or laughing at a
   whispered joke, they are laboring against a deadline or wasting the
   clock, and after a manager has surveilled the cubicles and returned to
   his office, their hands are still holding pens that must ultimately leave
   marks of anger and desire and calculation.

~

In a class I was teaching at a literacy center, I was talking about some sen-
   tences, some lines of a poem, some feelings, and interrupting me a
   tired woman of about thirty-five began to speak to me urgently, I lis-
   tened, her face showed the intensity of a struggle within herself,

But what could she do? how could I help her? she said, if from as early as she
   could remember, for her whole life, nobody had told her *nothing*?

Nothing. Her strong somehow crooked face, her chipped tooth. Her solitary
   path to this moment—we all understood that she had come all this
   way without mother or father.

And an older woman sitting next to her put an arm around her after she had
   asked the unanswerable questions and together they cried softly.

Softly I said the word that I had learned was her scarred name,

Betty, I said, What you have just asked us all, this is what you know, this is
   what you have in yourself to tell us, to give to us, that we need.

In cold spring air

In cold
          spring air the
white wisp-
          visible
breath of
          a blackbird
singing—
          we don't know
to un-
          wrap these blind-
folds we
          keep thinking
we are
          seeing through

Rich pale pink

Rich pale pink and
        peach, clear like
watercolor
        washes, or
glowing thick on
        the lumpy
undersides of
        clouds against
dry widening blue
        of eastern
sky at late-March
        dawn, begin-
ning to reveal
        gray streets, roofs
gray, blue-gray, brown,
        and inter-
laced bare top elm
        branches, sun-
light arrives; at
        dusk, like a
delayed visual
        answer that's
been pondered for
        ten hours, come
the same colors,
        but different
feelings, as rich
        streaks peach, pink,
orange, crimson,
        against cold
withdrawing blue.
        I praise this
spectacle that
        makes me small
at our two back-
        of-the-house

upstairs windows,
               through which in
silence I can
               ponder the
empty yards of
               our neighbors—
ordinary
               dignity
of daily life
               scruffily
perfected by
               the absence
of everyone,
               the dead cars,
toys lying side-
               ways for a
season, a child's
               cap flung down
this afternoon,
               all at once
the day has passed,
               they're home now
from work, school, play,
               everyone
whom we missed or
               who is hurt-
ing us is here
               or absent,
supper is brought
               from ancient
kitchens, the night
               sky, cloudy
or clear, bears off
               its losses,
lets its bright spheres
               glow, withstands
our unconscious-
               ness of them.

Where moon light angles through

Where moon light angles
                through the east-west streets,
down among the old-
                for-America
tall buildings that changed
                the streets of other
cities, circulate
                elevated trains
overhead shrieking
                and drumming, lit by
explosions of sparks
                that harm no one, and
the shadowed persons
                walking underneath
the erratic waves—
                not of the lake but
of noise—move through fog
                sieved by the steel mesh
of the supporting
                structures or through rain
that rinses pavements
                and the el platforms
or through new snow that
                quiets corners, moods,
riveted careers.
                Working for others
with hands, backs, machines,
                men built hard towers
that part the high air;
                women and men built,
cooked, cleaned, delivered,
                typed and filed, carried
and delivered, priced
                and sold. The river
and air were filthy.

In a hundred years
builders would migrate
                north a mile but in
those modern times this
                was all the downtown
that was. And circling
                on a round-cornered
rectangle of tracks
                run the trains, clockwise
and counter, veering
                through or loop-the-loop
and out again. Why
                even try to list
the kinds of places
                men and women made
to make money? Not
                enough of them, yet
too many. From slow
                trains overhead some
passengers can still
                see stone ornaments,
pilasters, lintels,
                carved by grandfathers,
great uncles and gone
                second cousins of
today—gargoyle heads
                and curving leaves, like
memorials for
                that which was built to
be torn down again
                someday, for those who
got good wages out
                of all this building
or were broken by
                it, or both, yet whose
labor preserves a
                record of labor,

imagination,
>ambition, skill, greed,
folly, courage, cost,
>error, story, so
that a time before
>remains present with-
in the dark spark-lit
>loud careening now.

In an old cabinet

In an old cabinet I found
                something fine and long forgotten—
small carved chess pieces inside a
                dark wood box, they belonged to my
uncle Witaly Jakob—but
                in America called "V.J."
for Vitale Jacques, also "Vit"—
                who lived fast: the first child, born just
before his parents quit Russian
                Poland on their wandering way
here. His ear heard American,
                he raced his piano through silent-
film houses and white-jass bands, made
                recordings, rebelled against both
his TB and his doctors, in
                1929 he died, his
Gershwin, his New Orleans club life
                and two-hand speed ended, and this

wood box, once in his orbit, now's
                among the many live objects
arrayed around me (as around
                every lucky remembering
person) like the rock lumps and ice
                chunks trailing the wide-orbiting
head of a fast-moving comet.

And even though I see on the
                inside of the lid of the knife-
wrought wooden chess set Witaly's
                initials inscribed by his hand
with a twentieth-century
                pencil that newly sharpened gave

off that still unchanged dry scent of
                 baked wood and graphite as Vit held
it—I see it, I see you, Vit—
                 and even though my gravity

keeps him with me, holds close the things
                 I write on when I write them on-
to pieces of paper with a
                 pencil, yet his chess set is one
more item that some day no one
                 will identify or care to
keep, an object the meaning of
                 which will evaporate when we
do or burn with unheard flame at
                 the end of our revolutions.

Ode: At a twenty-four-hour gas station

At a twenty-four-hour gas station and garage and dingy Food Mart on a city
   corner of unending traffic, next door to a chain restaurant that serves
   breakfast and inert heavy pie all day and night,

Around cold midnight, around the front end of my car with its hood up,
   five young guys from Mexico, not like me, their fathers could be on
   farms, are crowding in, staring at the workings, and the knowing
   one, after an hour and a half of waiting for the replacement parts to
   be delivered and after having worked on other cars in the meantime,
   teaching the others,

Is replacing the busted radiator, more for his audience than for me, and I
   remember seeing

Seeing in Mexico, not like here, a market where beside each stall of alert
   flowers on display for those who walked by, and beside each pyramid
   of wakeful mangos, papayas, tomatoes, bananas, oranges, peppers,
   sat the one who sold them, a human representative of both bounty
   and deprivation, of commerce and labor, waiting,

But here the one who sells his labor must not wait,

And waiting, I in my turn have come out to see what's happening, I've gone
   back inside, I've pissed in the grimy men's room, I've come out again,
   I've gone back over my resolutions and regrets, out of nowhere I've
   felt that familiar pang of longing for someone loved who is else-
   where, I'm checking my watch,

The other guys are watching, joking, not wearing enough clothes against this
   chilling world, and unpaid, they're learning,

I'm learning how knowledge is passed on so that more young men can make
   some money with their hands,

You can make money with your hands, your speed, your back or your brain,
and with what's between the truth and a lie, what's between your legs,
you can make money,

Money was not the first thing on my mind long ago

When I was young, for me learning was something in books, books were
not inert but sometimes would seem about to beat like wings in my
hands, I wanted all the books I could get and I thought that enough
money would somehow come,

It comes in steadily here to the two owners, partners, Italian, not like me,
they preside in shifts over the garage, the half-empty store, the
cooked coffee, "Free" says the sign, in a dusty half-empty carafe
on a hot hot plate, over the grimy restrooms and the space beside
them, a kind of waiting room—

Three waiting beat-up conjoined seats transplanted from some failed theater.

~

I go inside and sit down for a while longer in an end seat, and in the other
one now, one empty seat between us, is an old man, not like me, I
saw him earlier talking with the night-owning Italian, he's resting
both his big hands on a hand-carved cane with a wooden handle
shaped like a dull axe blade, he's wearing a Greek hat at a jaunty or
negligent slant,

You dress good, he says to me, but I'm wearing nothing special, and because
so often I feel on guard against others, that's the way I learned to be,
I had deliberately not greeted him with my eyes as he watched me,

Now his accent tells me he's from here, because

Here is a place of eighty different accents, a city neighborhood of ugly and
not expensive two-flats and six-flats and frame houses, houses of
mixed plans for the future and of families finished and dispersed,

of old worlds that don't fit, of children who love their grandparents
and are ashamed of them, of short sprees and long hard hours, of
dwellings corroded by the blowing urban exhalations,

Breathing hard, here some men and women have escaped a mortality else-
where—Little Rock or Sarajevo—or have fallen across oceans from
Saigon or Beirut into a mortality here, the storefronts speak

In tongues, the air is thick with speech, with grime, mistaken beliefs, odors
of commercial cooking, gasoline, this is city air, and

And the old man, a city creature, wants conversation and

And to save my mortal soul for a few minutes, I turn to him and yield
my gaze,

Guess, he says, where I'm from, You'll never guess.

~

I guess Poland and he's startled but also pleased that he has not stumped me,

He stamps the cane and tells me his story

(Part of it: Jewish, he survived, he doesn't tell me how, he stayed in Warsaw
till the 1950s, a tailor, he came to this country, to Chicago—Like
coming through door, he says, I think I understand what he means—
and he worked for years in clothing, he brought this cane all the way
with him, he takes it wherever he goes, nowadays he has a big stall in
a weekend flea market, keeps everything stored out there during the
week, has good quality clothes, Come see, he lives two blocks from
here, every evening he leaves his wife, she doesn't go out anymore, he
comes over here to the garage, he sits for an hour or two and drinks
the bad free coffee, even late at night he talks with anyone who might
sit down near him to wait),

This place is all there is in this part of the world for him to use

The way he once used cafés in Warsaw

(In Warsaw, before his escape from those systems of bureaucracies of fear,
 he could not have foreseen this system's negligence and its clamoring
 transmitted voices and fantastic products and incrustations of fan-
 tasy but he hoped for livelihood and found it),

Cardin, Claiborne, Calvin Klein, Tommy, he says proudly, You save money,
 Is biggest flea market, hundreds vendors, Ev'ryt'ing, Come see good
 clothes on weekend, You coming?

I tell him one part of my story: not from Warsaw but from Lodz and before
 that, Bialystok, came my maternal Jewish grandparents, a hundred
 years ago, I was right, he says proudly, I say you look like man from
 Europe,

So I say, Half of me,

And I see my father's young ghost running away again from the Mississippi
 farm of his Irish father and half-Choctaw mother and I see his old
 ghost backing away from this conversation and I ask the old man,
 What's your name?

Bill, he says, he smiles, and an unkempt, easy-gaited man of thirty or so, not
 like me or Bill, carrying an already disordered section of a news-
 paper, comes past us and without trying the doorknob of the men's
 room he goes straight into the ladies'—Bill and I hear distinctly the
 click of the lock

~

And we look at each other, I'll be back, I say, and I go out to the garage and
 the fifth young man is still working on the radiator, explaining to
 the other four what he's doing, they all smile at me, they're shivering
 and laughing and talking shit at each other, again I think of or am
 thought by someone far away whom I miss and want to see again,
 right now,

When Bill sees me coming back he tilts his head toward the ladies' room and
    raises his eyebrows to tell me the guy is still in there, and as soon as I
    sit down again a young woman comes past us, her face showing her
    distress, not like mine,

She's dressed inexpensively but very nicely, with smart shoes, I see that
    Bill has appraised her clothes, anyone would say she has a beauti-
    ful mouth, she comes past us and then the locked doorknob of the
    ladies' stops her, she glances at us in embarrassment, in need, The
    men's is empty, I say politely to her and she looks offended that I have
    spoken to her at all and she retreats out of sight

And Bill sighs, shrugs his shoulders at me, says, Do you believe?

Men once believed in gods, I say,

That's true, he answers, But anything can be doorway, if you give it push:
    working with hands—you see dese hands?—; or philosophy; or
    seeing people around you suffer; or piece of epple pie; or live with
    your own t'oughts, day after day where you don't see no one else has
    t'oughts like that; or even clothes . . .

Or a woman's beautiful mouth? or five young men talking in Spanish around
    a radiator at midnight? I ask,

And Bill says, Yes, of course! Or cane!—and he raises this dark worn wooden
    object so that I will see that on the handle, the head, are a dozen little
    jangling tarnished rings on tiny posts, the cane seems almost capable
    of knowing; of seeing; or even speaking,

Then we hear the toilet flushing and the guy comes out, no longer carrying
    the newspaper, and he saunters away,

The bad dust on everything is like powdered herbs of neglect and death-
    money,

I can smell the cheap thick cooked coffee,

The young woman returns rushing into the ladies', the faithful door offers
 the guarantee of its locking click, library-ships that were intended to
 arrive at faraway places of no books are sinking, the mass media are
 a junkyard of new cars, and the miners are lying sick in their shacks,
 money comes first, everything is the same as always and always
 changed, lilies or papayas or midnight repairs, blue jeans or stories,
 and in this moment as in every moment there is some possibility that
 the last moment did not have, some other jalapeño or orchid or high
 heel, some other radiator repair, some other young man who has left
 home to find work,

And Bill is looking at me, and every messianic, apocalyptic or ordinary hour
 of night and day, like this hour, seems infinite,

I ask him, Why are you here so late tonight, Bill? Don't you usually go home
 by now?

The Italian on duty hastens across the cement Food Mart floor into the
 garage, loudly calling one of his workers, Bill and I watch him,
 Chicago is not like Italy or Mexico or Poland but Poland, Mexico
 and Italy are here in the garage, I know and I don't understand this,

Bill holds out his wrinkled heavy hand

To shake my hand, to offer and to receive honor and acknowledgment, we
 have mortal souls

And our souls need continual repair,

Don't know why, Bill says—Workings of whole earth, I t'ink about, they keep
 me up in middle of night—clothes, bills, what newspapers say, then
 if I sleep I have bad dream, no, is good to sit here longer, talk, till you
 go. Then I go.

The young woman did office work

The young woman did office work,
                wore short skirts and heels, made herself
up, in very still morning when
                I was a hybrid of boy and
some creature without kind, she would
                step out of the rented place, walk
through the coarse dew-damp grass across
                our back yard, come out the clanking
gate in our chain-link fence, tiptoe
                past the outside wall of the bed-
room my brother and I shared, get
                with flashing leg into her trashed
Ford, she and her husband, unlike
                most, even poor, Texans, only
owned one old car between them, parked
                it to the side of our concrete
drive on crushed-shell gravel Daddy
                had had hauled in by groaning dump-
truck and poured onto the living
                grass, and she—young woman older
than I—would back, turn around, inch
                crunching out past our obstructing
bushes, bend forward to look, hit
                the gas, and I would let go of
the window blinds I had risen
                to push just a little apart.

On sad suburban afternoons of autumn

On sad suburban afternoons of autumn,
                    the piercings, leather and tattoos that bought
these bungalows from mixing bowls and golf
                    barbeque and drink beer, watch football, eat,
laugh like ponies—everything has changed
                    and not a lot except which music blares
through the meat-scented smoke and streaks of sun.
                    Big motorcycles drip dark staining oil
where Oldsmobiles once waited between breakdowns.
                    Slightly aslant on windows are the self-
adhesive souvenirs of stadium concerts
                    by rockers getting osteoporosis;
T-shirts advertise five-pointed leaves;
                    kids are neglected in the age-old ways,
unkempt and shrieking as they run—or older,
                    buy their own weed, sneak drinks, ditch school and fuck.
In front yards, back yards, alleys and dead ends
                    may all these signs convince the distant gods—
or Fate, or The Fates, an absent "G–d," a Christ
                    somewhere or other, not right here, an Allah
with gnashing prophets, or a great magician,
                    or the chance events that can destroy a life—
that there's no need to bring down any more
                    than customary miseries and brief
illusions of good luck on such old, young,
                    different, same, frail creatures of a day.

Celebration

The workday's over and
              three stools away from me
in the noisy bar-and-
              cheap-seafood-joint I want
to enjoy, a blind man—
              white hair, shabby good clothes,
a man led to what seems
              his customary place
by the young clear-eyed good-
              looking hostess—has lit
a half cigarette, drawn
              the drug in, is sipping
a draft beer, his lips smile;
              we wait; as I'm listening
to and writing down what,
              even if finally use-
less, I must try to think
              through after I transcribe
it from my small machine,
              the blind man, who can't know
what I'm doing, brings out
              of a pocket his own
recorder and in its
              ear whispers his own sound-
notes and I can't know what
              they are or what they're for.
Am I writing down the
              words that he is saying?

Amid loud talk and T
              V, clatter of service,
the sightful bartender
              brings each of us a bowl
of green-herbed memory

and fish as intricate
in flavor as is thought
in echoes, places, grace-
notes, associations,
in recognitions and
repressions. Shaped in each
day's events, reshaped by
each day's wishes, wrongs, needs.
Our hunger feeds on wit-
ness, wants to sit down with
friends and allies. Even
while eating by myself
I feel a welcome I
had not expected, and
after he has his word
I want to give a friend
who works and comes here blind
from his hard good thought bread.

Ode: Sometimes there's neither sun nor shadow

Sometimes there's neither sun nor shadow, mist closes behind me, here or
there stands someone in the fields, eyes closed, recalling and trying
to be recalled.

Daddy's close sister tried to lead me by my hand toward her hardshell
religion when I was a boy, but I resisted, and when I say with my
memory's voice her name, "Aunt Berta," it is with Daddy's accent
that I still sometimes call her Aint Berta—the way I said her name
as a child without ever hearing the language play in my saying that
she was not who I was saying she was.

And if she wasn't, how would I remember her, so many years later, when she
would be gone?

A mist-cloud with no head comes in from the Gulf of Mexico rolling its
many shoulders,

Against it women and men stand up in the sea-side fields and succeed in
some of their efforts to recall, and say softly a few things.

Even though the mist makes everything difficult to remember.

Such as: my father's hands—reassuring, threatening.

When in this time, not in the past, I see a young mother hold her infant
girl upright by tiny hands so the baby can try her first steps across
the rug, I think of the word that these hands speak and that the
mother hears one way, the daughter, who will not remember this,
another way,

And I try to not forget my dead father, that is, I try to bring something more
of him back to mind, some gesture of his that spoke to me,

I recall him or call to him.

When the sound of that infant girl's crying wanders faintly among these
houses of my neighborhood, I think how someday, long after having
left home, she will see old photos of this new moment and will try to
find the lost name for it,

As I now try to find a name for the long-forgotten but photographed mo-
ment when my father caught me falling down into his hands from
the thousand-foot height to which he had thrown me,

Maybe laughing out my name.

~

His speech always remained soft—it was a long-ago hardshell farmstead
Mississippian Baptist and in fact pleasant to the ear.

I would hear him yell at me, or at other times, for me, as I was thrown from
a green horse that he had bought cheap and wanted me to clean up
for him, it needed to be well mannered, so he could make a couple
hundred dollars when he sold it,

Horses he himself never rode, and I hit the ground mostly unhurt, and he
would yell at me to get back on, and only many years later did I learn
that my father (who had waited till I myself was heavy with age to
tell me this) had been an easy rider, jumping fences bareback on that
poor farm of his boyhood.

I waited many years for that disclosure, since he did not tell things, but more
often lived in quiet; or silenced—

When I knew him, the habitual set of his face when he was preoccupied,
when he tilted his half-black-Irish head back slightly and puzzled
at something or bore up under it, gave the long-sunned darkness of
his face, the reserve of his mouth and his straight wide nose and the
angles of his part-Choctaw cheekbones an unintended remoteness,

Doubly dispossessed, although

He knew a little of the language of horses, and he could talk authoritatively
at a mule, a calf, roosters and hens.

I would look out a back window at him when at dusk he stood in our broad
hot back yard on the inland coastal Texas plains, holding a green
hose and spraying water here and there on the grass, saying with
this gesture, "I am alone."

In old age he would begin to speak by saying, "In other words . . ." and could
not entirely say what he was seeing and in some way had already said,
comprehensibly or not, within himself, somehow,

Or there were some things he never did comprehend nor find other words for.

I can hear, voiced by my body but not by my conscious sense of myself, a
certain way of clearing my throat, a timbre, a tone, that I think I
recognize as his—how he sounded when he was younger than I am
now and I was a boy about to leave home,

As if he, scarcely ever—that I knew—having spoken for or spoken up for
himself, were still trying to speak, but this time through me.

Am I recalling myself? Or is this one of the ways I am not who I am.

~

A name-word may be a changeable word and a false name, flashing like an
escaping fish—but after having struggled to find it, even sometimes
to catch it bare-handed, I am not going to give it up.

I am not going to wish that every thing in the world might be returned to its
maiden name

(There's always an earlier one, in all languages the old new words wait in
irregular ranks to be said once more,

And not even they are capable of voicing all the relations

Of selves to themselves and to each other and to the things we hear and see),

But I do wish for a better unforgetting,

I try to not forget my father, that is, to call a little more of him back to mind,
    although if I ask myself what about him in myself comes to me, it
    might be not reassurance but a threat—

Like when I was seven or eight, with other men and another boy, my father
    and I went out in a shining brown wooden boat onto the waters of
    the Gulf to fish for sand trout and he made a frightening joke about
    what he and the other men baiting hooks would use if they ran out
    of their chopped bait,

And I'm sure I looked away and tried to seem like a good fisherboy, but I
    caught nothing,

And after the fishing, the owner of the boat, one of Daddy's bosses, when
    running fast toward shore aslant the big waves as the weather came
    up brought the boat, and again I was afraid, repeatedly near capsizing
    as with his will he laughed and drove it against the waves and when
    it tried to cut each one at an angle with its prow it shuddered and
    yawed sharply, throwing us against each other.

A thousand-foot fall from a boat, from a horse . . .

~

Talking too much, I eventually left Dad and went out the road away from my
    youth, alone—

And if we could throw ourselves into the right arms, but we can't,

Then the abyss at the side of the bed in which we try to sleep, a thousand-
    foot fall,

Would seem easy to overleap.

~

When I departed from Texas guiltily, giddily I did not think I ever would
      return to live there, and I did not want to turn and see behind me
      Daddy and Mother waving goodbye to me from inside my forehead.

I had outgrown beatings, or he had, and so I would miss his tentative smile
      and his laconic, almost bashful, words.

I imagined him standing in a field of his childhood, I imagined him
      straightening his tired young back after a while of reaching for
      the low cotton.

Aint Berta is there, too, it's before school, above them birds are crossing the
      sky through the wind like something that something is saying that
      can't be heard.

But I was forever leaving, and when at times I did look back, the shadow I
      was throwing said nothing and it was wearing a Western hat with a
      snakeskin band that I was not.

I watched the snake crawl away.

Houston's old snaking trailways were exaggerating their reach with millions
      of tons of concrete, thick-stalked skyscrapers were rising from a
      squat, lights were spreading far under the night in steady hurricanes
      of electricity, and by day Dad was out there driving his little truck,
      working . . .

Now that the sun is low, I stand at the top of his long powerless shadow,
      unavoidably on its chest or its face.

I have departed over and over, I am leaving again when I work at these
      simple words.

My Herakleitos

In memory of Timothy Dekin

1.

I open a small book and work
                at understanding, so that from
Kallimakhos, who lived
                four ages ago—and
from the succession of
                scholars and poets who
preserved his lines—I receive
                a brief remembrance that has
escaped time and war-
                lords, fire and ruin:

                "Someone spoke of what happened to you, Herakleitos.
                "This brought me to tears and recalled how you and I,
                "Sitting outside, would talk the sun all the way down.
                "But for a long time, my friend from Halikarnassos,
                "You have been ashes. Your poems still sing—that plunderer,
                "Death, will not get his hands on those."

2.

They are gone, those nightingales
                of that Herakleitos, but
I use the old poem to
                make a new remembrance:

Someone spoke of what
                happened to you, Tim,
and this brought me to tears
                and recalled to me how

in a coffee house or later
             when you half sat, half lay on your
living-room couch and your rented
             oxygen generator was
never not buzzing at the
             end of a long thin clear tube,
we would talk till the day
             grew dark outside. Gone from
the realm of the living, you,
             born in what city I don't
remember, have been
             ashes for a long
year—like some
             destroyed place.

But that monster of plunder,
             Forgetting—however much
we ourselves help him,
             however much he
carries off, approved by the rage,
             the zeal, the greed and laughter of
all those who conquer us—will
             not get his hands on your poems.

3.

They are still with
             us, your poems, Tim,
but I can't know
             for how long. You
praise neither the accomplices
             of power nor those who resist
it; your poems memorialize
             no conquerors or rebels and
neither sort will
             notice your poems.

At miniatures like yours
                and mine, we work as though we
mistakenly wished to
                honor or appease gods;
we labor at fine detail as
                though with mouse-whisker brushes, like
Persian painters long
                forgotten—because
in this way we revive some-
                thing old that we believe to
be always good.
                Kallimakhos
remembers his friend,
                and you remembered
Kallimakhos, and
                I remember you.

                4.

Man-made god-storms burn through cities and families.
The great god Malice grows with the worship given to him.
The great god Forgetting kicks with satisfied contempt
at the heaps of ashes left behind by his clanging armies.

                5.

Your words, Tim, breathed
                aloud into
my speech or anyone's,
                are again and again
as alive as mulberries. (Greek,
                which uses no rhyming in its
ancient poems, can make Fate
                and those shining berries

a half-rhyme we can sing
                    against ash of cafés
and books, ash of friends,
                    even of twilights.
But just as alive as
                    indigo mulberries
are your words
                    when I or
anyone breathes them back
                    into live speech again.)

2003

Enough

Walking in a small park,
I ask myself what to
think of Thebes, Leeds, Baghdad,
Dacca, Lagos, Lhasa,
Rome, Prague, Perth, La Paz, Guam,
Ho Chi Minh, Pskov, Lodz, Durg,
Dresden, Elabuga.

~

Constant splashing of the
fountain—shapeless water
thrown from beaks of iron birds,
tall cranes, into the all
ways yielding air, air strong
enough, though, to carry
on its bright back the scents
of yellow, red, peach, pink
petals on this cloudy
morning of cool summer,
the white light is wrong, it
is sifting down as slow
as snow, church bells, nine times,
make a dull comforting
sound but cannot make sense.

~

Alone till now, I hear
others nearby, and led
into this flower park
by her grandmother comes
on tiptoe a pale small
girl with straight red hair, in
a fine blue dress and white

stockings and shiny shoes,
they're red, too, abruptly
        she pulls her hand free, with
her own flourishing she
        prances ahead on the
as yet untrodden, art-
        fully raked gravel walk,
she's enough for herself.

~

I yield to her her place,
        retreat to a bench that
says who it remembers,
        as I'm always doing,
the little girl laughs with
        joy at the cranes, joy's real,
the water and cranes real,
        among these quiet streets,
in the midst of lucky
        houses never damaged.

Sleepless in the cold dark

Sleepless
     in the cold dark,
I look
     through the closed dim
door be-
     fore me, which be-
comes an
     abyss into
which my
     memories have
fallen
     past laughter or
horror,
     passion or hard
work—my
     memories of
our past
     laughter, horror,
passion,
     hard work. An ache
of be-
     ing. An ache of
being,
     over love. An
ache of
     being over
love. Like
     projections on
the screen
     of the heavy
window
     curtains, flashing
lights of

       a slow-scraping

after-

       midnight snowplow

for a

       moment pulse in

this room.

Ode: Samaritan

. . . going down from Jerusalem to Jericho . . .
—LUKE 10: 30–37

Just outside the city walls, yet again I came upon a person, this one

In his artisan's booth—it was framed of weathered dark thick beams of wood
built against the ancient stone that belonged to everyone

And no one,

He was standing at the open entrance under a sign that announced only
his name,

In some language or other that I knew and didn't know, "Tigerman,"

And in fact I wondered at first if somehow he

Was a tiger—his peculiar strong bare arms were striped by some inconceiv-
able feral gene or affliction of the skin, and his round face

Had an almost feline configuration of the nose and mouth, or seemed to
have, his assistant,

I thought it was, at first, wore a belt of chain but in fact it was a kind of leash
attached to a brutal spike

That had been driven decisively into the stone back wall of the booth, and
his misshapen head

Could not help with anything, and his right hand was withered, his legs were
stout and slow, but at the limit of his leash and being

He smiled and stayed near the tiger man, his guardian,

Who constructed and offered for sale to the occasional tourist

His small sculptures of black wrought iron, twisted and bent to resemble
      somewhat abstract figures

Of animals and men and women,

Unlike any such art of making I had ever before seen, and then a grandfather
      wearing the faded uniform of a soldier,

With gray hair and short beard and black eyes—I thought perhaps he was
      an Akkadian

Or Kurd, a former dragoman or a Babylonian or Afghani

Who had fled west—stopped to watch the artisan

Set up a small side space using two more of the heavy wood beams—
      evidently a kind of temporary annex where he could create his
      symbols

And which he would break down again each day after he

Had made and sold a few pieces of this craft—and the older man, the
      stranger,

Without speaking bent down quickly behind the tiger man

To volunteer his remaining strength to help lift the next beam, one end of
      which the tiger man

Had hefted already above his head, and the old man lifted his end high but
      the tiger man

Was startled by this unrequested aid behind him, had not understood what
      wordlessly his fellow creature—

Perhaps some former artisan himself, or former cat—was doing for him

And because of his own sudden surprised movement in response to that of
      the old foreigner

The lifeless beam slipped from the older man's still strong hands striking him
in the head and knocking him down and the tiger man with alarm
and anger heaved the whole evil

Beam to one side and leapt to undo too late the wound but the casualty

Lay awkwardly pushing himself

Backwards in the dirt and away, trying to lift himself with one arm,

Not bleeding but confused and harmed, and a graceful woman

Came out from among the hurrying, burdened, mostly oblivious pedestrians,

She knelt and when she noticed that his black eyes seemed to see with a
different gaze or not to see at all, she

Pressed him down, her touch urging him to remain very still—until, I hoped,
rescuers

Could arrive. And then the simple ward

Of the tiger man, fighting his unyielding leash in order to see, to get near him

Who was hurt, began to make an anguished sound that I

Am unable to describe, and I stood listening in awe as from his mouth, from
his head, from his poor body,

There came a sound that filled the narrow street around us

As the chained man was reaching toward the fallen elder, filled with the need
to help, would-be Samaritan—

But one unable ever to know to breathe into the child

Pulled from the sea or to know how to nurse the traveler

Who has been attacked or to protect the mother

Walking home at too late an hour, unable to save from error

That hapless citizen who stubbornly, with the ballot before him, invites the
rule of his tyrant.

And in my mind

I rushed away. Perhaps finally weeping, as the tiger man tried to help, to
watch over, to hold close, to calm, his good ward,

Who was tearing at himself in his pain of compassion.

These sideways leaps, remembering

These sideways leaps, remembering.
    A worn red chair's dignified still-
ness in a ranch-house mud room where
    a clock was always counting out
the lifetimes of horses. A big
    shabby one-floor gray-blue house on
12-foot stilts near the Gulf where the
    faithful took kids for a weekend
of Bible study but we all
    ran through the damp salt air at dusk
laughing even though the teachers
    called us. Live possum young hissing
on their dead mother's back. With our
    guns we shot armadillos. Out
of white smoke from a grassfire I
    had caused came a man appearing
and walking toward me, I thought, but
    going past me to get water
to drink. At Mother's slow, clinky
    spinet, I tried to quicken what
I could do with Bach's "Italian
    Concerto." My father turned his
weary green 1952
    car into our driveway (none of
this happens anymore) (did it
    ever happen?), he braked, cut the
engine, swung open the dull door
    and wearing his hat he got out.

Confession

Down in the blue-green water
          at nightfall some selving shapes
float fluorescing, trance-dancing,
          trembling to the rhythm of
theodoxical marching-
          music that they hear over
the mere noise of the breaking
          tide. Above, stars in certain
places; along the shore roads,
          cars carrying people on
uncertain errands, sordid
          and sacred and all the kinds
in between. Halogen-lit,
          a woman gets down from her
all-wheel-drive velocipede,
          enters through an obeying
door a cyclopean store
          to buy unintelligent
fresh fish and other objects
          whether formerly alive
or formerly dead, she comes
          out again, a poor man calls
to her, selling his no-news-
          paper; the disastrous head-
lines smile and nod, they announce
          the plans of steel patriots
and undertakers, ad-men
          and fallen vice-generals,
doping their stolen crusades.
          But the woman has learned, as
I have learned, as all of us
          must keep learning if we are

to be good subjects, how to

        make of a newspaper the

mask of a locust, calmly

        put it on, and begin once

more to eat everything up.

An aching young man

An aching young
                man on the street
approaches, stops
                me with his eyes
and saying Sir?
                Sir? he shows me
his right hand, it's
                purple and red,
blood-spotted, gro-
                tesquely swollen,
he says he fell
                while chasing a
thief who'd grabbed his
                backpack, with his
wallet in it,
                he has to get
home by bus to
                Carbondale, he
needs sixty-five
                dollars, he has
fifty, he shows
                me, his jaw moves,
What about the
                emergency
room? I ask, Man,
                he says, I don't
have a thousand
                for that bill, What
about pain pills,
                Advil, something?
I ask, he says
                That's eight dollars
for a bottle
                right there, he is
pressing his left

                    thumb deep into
the soft water-
                    balloon scabbing
mess of his harmed
                    right hand, he says
Man, this hurts, it
                    feels better when
I press on it,
                    Don't do that, I
say, but I don't
                    know anything,
why do I say
                    it except his
hand looks so bad
                    I don't see how
he'll recover?—
                    A nurse, he says,
she told me if
                    it's this swollen
then it isn't
                    broken it's frac-
tured You know what
                    time it is?—in
the face of his
                    logic I hold
out no alter-
                    natives, I hold
up my unharmed
                    right hand to show
him my watch, he
                    says, I can't see
it, and I tell
                    him it's two, I
ask myself why
                    can't he see it?
and he says My
                    bus is at five

then I live an

        hour and a half

on the other

        side of that Got

to get back to

        Kentucky, while

a nearby bill-

        board keeps showing

us both an ad,

        a visage half

woman and half

        leopard, a face

this age wrongly

        puts on fortune,

maybe, wronging

        the woman, the

leopard, and us,

        and in the row

of courageous

        trees that live and

die down the side-

        walk, a wind is

shoving the leaves

        this way and that.

Ode: I had been reading ancient Greeks

I had been reading ancient Greeks and digging, behind my house, and I
     had learned that Plato, even though he was no friend of storytelling,
     conceded that poetry, just like philosophy, arises

Arises out of the feeling of wonder

Wonder: philosophy and poetry flowing like a kind of water down river
     courses of human

Human experience, which changes over time, so thinking and feeling
     change, too, the way water of some endless river that will never reach
     any sea passes through narrow rocky rapids

Rapids but also smooth broad channels, running heroically or angrily, or
     peacefully or somehow horribly . . .

~

In spring the snow-melt around where I lived sometimes used to raise the
     water table so high that

That a backyard water-well like ours, sunk not very deeply into a gentle
     limestone slope, became

Became temporarily a spring because the precious, pressured underground
     water would rise

Would rise along the narrow well-shaft up past the buried electric pump and
     then it fountained when it came through

The surface of the earth, it "artesians," people there say, and then the water
     would fall

Would flow down again just a few feet further, following the slope of the
     yard, and would soak its way under the masonry sill of our old small
     house and flood

It would flood the dirt-floored crawl space underneath, so finally I

So I went out carrying a spade and in the very soft, mulchy, soggy, spring-
time soil under the big spruce near the back corner of our house I
began digging a trench a foot wide and a foot and a half deep

But less deep as I approached the humble source, and the pooled water on
the miniature swamp land around the well began to drain away

It drained into the new trench I had made and as if it were excited at some
as yet unknown possibility it rushed off from sunlight to shade, to
where I had begun, to where I was letting gravity guide it, and when
the water had nowhere else to go, gradually it pooled over there

The artesianing water pooled as it always had, but this time not under our
house but over the roots of the spruce, instead, and it sank back into
the soil toward them

I changed the water's story so it would run toward them

~

The possible outcomes of choices already made make up the world of real
conditions now

But I can't make all the connections

The water would not have run to the spruce if I hadn't trenched the soft
spring earth, tossing heavy spadefuls of it under nearby cedars

It wouldn't have artesianed if the owners before me hadn't sunk the well

They wouldn't have dug the well if they hadn't needed water for the house
when the house was new to this spot, sixty years before—although
the house itself was not new, but already old, for during one winter in
the 1940s, men sledded the house over, across frozen Green Bay from
the other side

In the 1940s, they wouldn't have sledded the house if they hadn't had some
good reason, I don't know what it was, that made them want to go
that far to get it rather than build a new house where they wanted it

~

From reading a newspaper I learned that a young woman I knew from when
she was a girl of five and went to school with our girl, year after year,
till they both left their homes for colleges on opposite coasts of this
incomprehensible country, had been overcome

Overcome by the affliction of depression and self-isolation, she secretly
hanged herself down in a ravine in remote woods

In woods or meadows, in villages or cities, the good what-ifs are like wells
that were only imagined or desired and were in fact never imposed
by human will, never dug, never gave good water, and then their
absence rather than their presence was the next condition to which
some adjustment simply had to be made, by this person and that—
an old story

In the old story, the last living person of the family of Laios, two generations
after him, was the girl Ismene, whom poetry, even when telling this
story, simply leaves behind, as if nothing

Nothing she could say or do will be worth knowing after her fierce older sis-
ter, Antigone, herself perhaps only sixteen or eighteen years old, and
unmarried, and never to be a mother, has hanged herself inside the
underground chamber of a tomb

It was a tomb in which her tyrannical uncle, Kreon—himself a kind of
affliction that Antigone seemed doomed to bear—ordered her sealed
up alive with token food and water so that, to his way of thinking,
her death of thirst and starvation could not be blamed on him

And while he, the Kreon of ruling power and girl-hating, wears his mask of
unyieldingness, maybe inside us, among those several selves each of
us is, there is some other Kreon of the spirit who wears the mask of a
hounding hopelessness

~

Unable any longer to hope, yet opposed to our present-day Kreons and to
the Kreon who was loud within her, the poor girl in the tyrannical
news, who has died, was capable of dear, cherishable enthusiasms
and ideals and sympathies, for which friends say they loved her like
a sister

Ismene loved her sister Antigone

But Ismene said she could not follow Antigone, who herself was flowing
toward death, yet neither could Ismene think of how to live without
Antigone, and we

We can't connect things when we hear the news

Unwanted news of one girl's suffering and death pours across us, through us,
swamps us

There is no news at all of most of the girls hounded and harassed and hated,
and like this girl's absence

The absence of each of them—new absences keep arriving—is the reality to
which those people over there, or these nearby, all of us, must adjust
ourselves, instead of, for instance, to a girl's presence, we must think
of her

Her capacities that will not be realized, her stories that will not

~

I finished my digging

The trench kept the water from flowing into the dank crawl space under
the house, where it had made a pool that was I admit harmless but,
in that darkness we do not see, beneath the floor, the water seemed
sinister—water in the earth and under it, like the mythological black
river that Greeks believed they would cross to reach the dim after-
world where they would continue to exist but as shadows

~

The well water rising on its own that day purled harmlessly, flowing on its
    course of only a few feet into the shade, out of spring sunlight, float-
    ing bits of last year's dead leaf and grass on a quick buoyant little
    journey down new currents from here to a new place, a place made
    real and possible, from here to there—from here to there, that's it,
    that's all, that's enough—just as if

~

Just as, although the gravity of our lives conducts us downward, we—up
    through something like a guiding shaft toward air, toward some
    decisive act or new ideas or reprieve—we artesian for a while

And for a little while philosophy or poetry or overhearing the sound of a
    daughter's voice, somewhere nearby, restores wonder while we all
    are standing in our muddy back yards

~

As though the old story were instead that Antigone did marry—as she
    wanted—and received as her due the proper share of life that she
    wanted and deserved, and that she had children and they also flour-
    ished and made use of their gifts, holding to one another and to her
    and to their father while with love and wonder they became aware of
    a world new to them that—just as we want it to, for them, and for the
    girl who does not die by her own hand that has turned into the hand
    of Kreon—a world that awaits them all with at least its possible good.

Fern-Texts

Autobiographical Essay on the Notebooks of Young
Samuel Taylor Coleridge (b. 1772)

1.

Coleridge wrote of himself:

> There are two sorts of talkative fellows whom it would be injurious to
> confound
>
> & I, S. T. Coleridge, am the latter. The first sort is of those who use five
> hundred words more [than] there needs to express an idea—that is
> not my case—few men, I will be bold to say, put more meaning into
> their words than I or choose them more deliberately & discriminat-
> ingly. The second sort is of those who use five hundred more ideas,
> images, reasons &c than there is any need of to arrive at their object
>
> till the only object arrived at is that the mind's eye of the bye-stander
> is dazzled with colors succeeding so rapidly as to leave one vague
> impression that there has been a great Blaze of colours all about some-
> thing. Now this is my case—& a grievous fault it is
>
> my illustrations swallow up my thesis   [25 December 1804]

But begin with metaphor:

> Ginger to be sliced—Lemons to be peeled—The Sugar & Water to be
> boiled together, & the Scum—viz—the Monarchical part [—] must
> go to Pot—and out of the Pot—<u>Then</u> put in the Ginger with the Peels
> of the Lemons, and let the whole be boiled together gently for half
> an hour—When cold, put in the Lemon juice strained &c—then let
> the Sum total be put in the Barrel with three spoonfuls of Yeast—let
> it work three Days (Sundays Excepted—) and then put in a Gallon
> Barrel—Close up the Barrel—Nota bene—you may do it legally the
> habeas corpus act being suspended—let it remain a fortnight then
> bottle it.   [1795-6?]

(One could *tyrannically*

confine the fermenting stuff

because in '94 the

government had suspended

the right of persons not to

be jailed without being charged.)

2.

"Love transforms the souls into

a conformity with the

object loved—" and when I too   [1796?]

was twenty-four I had my   [1971]

own experience of such self-

transformation that I could

not yet seize or recognize—

experience of objects loved

but also feared, approving

and disapproving: women,

men, cities, books, ideas,

wearying labor, wild free-

dom in cars, America,

how a people should govern

themselves, and war; and I tried

to think or not think about

what seemed unthinkable since

it was so everyday: Dad

for instance, working out of

his car; Mother ordering

us all around and being

ordered at her job; drinking

fountains and restrooms marked for

race; barbed wire, teargas, school, church,

a book shop, ditches, weeds, rain;

often I had unconscious-

ly made myself adjust the

                    goal in myself that I could
not myself perceive but which
                    I longed to attain, reform-
ing it repeatedly in
                    order to discover what
it might be or might become.

                    He wrote: "An eminently
beautiful Object is Fern,
                    on a hill side, scattered thick
but growing single—and all
                    shaking themselves in the wind."   [August 1800]
"There have been times when looking
                    up beneath the shelt[e]ring Tree,
I could Invest every leaf
                    with Awe." From such words I make   [September 1803]
the Samuel who will to
                    me speak what I am able
to hear—a man excited
                    to notice, describe, and love
(no less than an explorer
                    of America) the free
expanses that come into
                    his view—in a landscape, in
an idea: they rise further
                    into sight with each step up-
ward over a difficult
                    pass, they rise with a kind of
magnificence we should not
                    call "majestic" (remember
monarchical sugar): the
                    view is of infinity,
as in the mere intricate
                    veins of a leaf or one tree
of leaves or in the rushing
                    stream of changeable feeling

at a farewell or a birth.

            I hold close in thought the work,
the writer, who will evoke
           in me what I want to be.

3.

Because of my own slow green
           passage toward freer thinking
I leave aside his hopes of
           Christianity (he'd be
horrified at this), and all
           the pretty rituals and
the austere, too, the willful
           ignorance and anger—yet
to say this in our culture
           is still to be subject to
denunciation by the
           theatrically faithful.
How willingly our denounced
           religions of conquest have
veered, how violent and how
           self-acquitting they have been,
with what agility they
           fix interpretation of
laws and signs they claim are theirs
           in war and violation.
Young faithfulness evoked in
           me something good. Bad too, no
surprise, especially hot
           certainties I heard professed
by those around me. To be
           evoked as I wanted to
be—those values too, half learned
           from unhappy churchgoing—
I needed to choose other
           thinking, others. "My nature

requires another nature

        for its support"—not systems   [November 1803]

of thought or belief but re-

        sponsive imagination

that becomes the very same

        puzzling "streamy Nature of

Association" that Sam

        believed "Thinking[, which] =

Reason[,] curbs & rudders." *Must*

        curb, since Association,

to him, is "the Origin

        of moral Evil." Like us   [December 1803]

he dreamed by day, following

        the pleasure or the trouble

of leaping from thought to thought,

        image to image. And he

himself knows that we grow up

        "from Infancy to Manhood

under Parents, Schoolmasters,

        Tutors, Inspectors," and more,

"having had our pleasures &

        pleasant self-chosen Pursuits

interrupted, & we forced"

        into what he says are "dull

unintelligible Rud-

        iments or painful Labor."   [10 January 1804]

What teachers and masters in-

        terrupted was his, our, soul-

making reverie, even

        ethics of choice and being

chosen by what both frees and

        affiliates us and gives

strength to leaping aid and calm

        compassion. But Coleridge

locates moral lapsing in

        the very reverie to

which he himself inclined, while

        at the same time he grasps how

he needs such streamy thinking
                    to form himself as a man
with a conscience pained by his
                    own failings. He wonders "when
men shall be as proud within
                    themselves of having remained
an hour in a state of deep
                    tranquil Emotion, whether
in reading or in hearing
                    or in looking, as they now
are in having figured a-
                    way one hour." One supposes   [10–11 January 1804]
he is abominating
                    tallies of profit and loss,
those figures, yet one does hear
                    in his way of putting it
his saying what the poet
                    does: a figuring. His plan
of self-improvement followed:
                    "1 Up—wash—ginger Tea hot.
2 Italian till Breakfast
                    Time. 3 Breakfast 4 Write or
transcribe my Journal. 5th read
                    the Theodicee & take
notes for my Consolations.
                    6th Then write my letters on
literary Detraction
                    or a review of Wordsworth";

he added: "in short, something,
                    beginning with this. 7th
between dinner & tea what
                    I can. Read some Italian
if possible. after tea
                    till bed time try to compose."

                    *

Final plea: "God grant me fort-
        titude & a persever-
ant Spirit of Industry!"—   [April 6, 1804]
        writing this while on a ship
bound for Malta and, he hoped,
        a position and an es-
cape from his misery at
        home: in love with a woman
not his wife and not in love
        with his wife, although yes dot-
ing on his small son and no
        not seeming to expect he'd
write more poems, and revising
        his own lived life history
as one who had acted a
        revolutionary (called
in England, "Jacobin") but
        now was deceiving others
and himself, defender of
        order and obedience,
God, sceptre, commentary.
        Increasingly an anti-
democratic man who'd come
        to hate those in whose name he'd
fought—yet he didn't have to
        like what common people did,
but only identify
        himself with their suffering,
no? He can't help but still *see:*

Wednesday, April 11, 1804
Sea & Sky, & an irregular circle of Ships of which we seem the Center.
Saw a nice black faced bright black-eyed white toothed Boy running
up to the Main Top with a large Leg of Mutton swung, Albatross-
fashion about his neck 'Rear'd' for a Ship lad, taught every thing by
Curses—yet well-behav'd the while, & his Master shed a tear when
he died—for the Boy would sing on the Top Mast, a Song neither of
Love nor of Wine, & come down with Tears on his Cheeks

(Was the boy's racing up the

                        mast to the main top merely

high spirits? Or could he have

                        been escaping in order

to eat in freedom the meat

                        he, so hungry, had stolen?

How did he happen to die?

                        For what reason did he die?)

The ethical—not only

                        to see but also to act.

    4.

C. wrote down that Poetry

                        might be "a rationalized

Dream dealing [?out] to mani-

                        fold Forms our own Feelings, that

never perhaps were attached

                        by us consciously to our

own personal Selves." The wit

                        of poems, their arguments, all

that age-old manner of how

                        thought might move reasonably

in them, he saw was at heart

                        a dreaming, with states and shifts

of feeling and image and

                        narratives moving with that

peculiar syntax of con-

                        nections that lie beneath what

we think we think. Wasn't this   [11 May 1804]

                        his own discovery that

writing makes possible an

                        understanding of how we

should act, could claim our selves, must
                            redeem our selves from the acts
by which we have pawned ourselves,
                            from the formation that we
mistakenly accepted
                            or helplessly accepted
(formation, though, that we are
                            continuing to accept,
it is so hard to resist)
                            as our servitude? Sailors
on several ships in his
                            convoy shot repeatedly
at an exhausted hawk that
                            tried to rest on the bowsprits,
that flew off each time but had
                            to return to alight on
one ship or another: "Poor
                            Hawk! O Strange Lust of Murder
in Man! It is not cruelty
                            it is mere non-feeling from
non-thinking." Pity for the
                            hawk, anguish; for the sailors
not distaste, hate or fear—he
                            who had envisioned the shoot-
ing of the albatross!—but
                            fellow-feeling, forgiveness.

5.

Co-creating with other
                            poets the new way in which
poetry in English would
                            mostly work, he perceived the
linguistic spirit which (be-
                            cause of the particular
history, customs, and thought

of the English—and he would

have understood these in yet

another way if his plans

of emigrating to this

America had not failed)

had made possible in past

poetry (and was feeding

the use by new poets of)

"rapid associations

of sensuous images,"

"rapid association

& combination both of

images with images,

& of images, & com-

binations of images[,]

with the moral and intel-

lectual world, and vice ver-

sa[,] words of passion and thought

with natural images."   [4–7 February 1805]

So that in him (and in Words-

worth) we see those first moments

of a perceiving that's an

act sufficient to itself—

we read their early work in

the hope that this perceiving

won't become a *substitute*

for their democratic hopes

and a retreat from their friends

who are being chased through the

shires by zealous, triumphant

reactionaries into

persecuted hiding, jail . . .

But already we know the

story—Coleridge and Words-

worth will change. Yet they saw that
the poetic perceiving
                    is of some object—thing or
place, prospect or person—and
                    that the perceiving of a
person is an attending
                    to particular features,
qualities: ordinary,
                    concrete, specific, worn, real.
Then a poem needs no appeal
                    to divine sanction, nor to
an aristocratic nor
                    even a middle-class sense
of propriety, it needs
                    image and narration, it
needs the evocation of
                    another human being
in individuated
                    encounter, the poem needs a
conviction of uniqueness
                    and a tone of voice as if
whispering praise and sorrow,
                    language attuned to spicules,
sepals and scars, to surprise
                    that pleasingly confounds ex-
pectation, an attentive-
                    ness that at least sometimes thrills
to the strange, the sublimely
                    peculiar and to the im-
ponderable and the un-
                    conscious—what's this?—a grasping

(flawed by its wanting to know
                    everything and to possess)

                    *

graspable—and once I too
                went naming things, sensations,
and extending sentences
                out to greater length as I
reached the wave-beaten New-World
                west coast, where syntax too seemed
a wave to be caught, ridden,
                "articulate energy,"
I started reading Duncan,
                Rexroth, Snyder, Neruda,
Wang Wei, Paz, streamy thinkers—
                did the nerve of a culture
that was dying need thunder
                to rouse it? (Everson). I
stood amidst war that was else-
                where and here, resistance, bliss,
paradise gardens, talk-fights,
                hot hearts, sobs and chants, stands on
streets against cops and fragrant
                stands of laurel on hillsides,
eucalyptus along roads,
                sloping apricot orchards,
avocets on the wide beach
                striding, beaking through each wave's
last thin rushing, and herons
                in treetop nests, terns diving
with tucked wings and spearpoint plunge,
                used books and records, new wine
sold cheap from old oak barrels,
                endless blossoming in yards,
woods, fields, gardens, bedrooms; and
                incense burning in the streets—
but now my illustrations
                will swallow up my thesis.
Which is: love capable of
                affiliation and in-
dependence: love that could speak

love, love that could brighten mind
"into conformity with":
                    a west-coast Black Mountain or
ocean chaotically
                    breaking against and into
rocks, caves, cliffs, thoughts, thoughts winging
                    fast as songbirds into mist
nets of larger ideas that
                    held for just a moment, near
wet seaside fields of pumpkins
                    incandescent in fog-glow . . .

Music (not my own) in the   [1971–72]
                    family carried me out:
sped by just enough resolve
                    and by money from L.A.
where Uncle Dan with fiddle
                    had earned it in studios
and airmailed a gift check—Go!—,
                    I lit out for the past, took
a long sea-journey: reading
                    Moby Dick in a sling chair
on the freight-deck, playing chess
                    with two old spinster sisters
who both beat me happily,
                    the course set not for Malta
but with cargo for Tangiers,
                    then Civitavecchia; then
after disembarkation
                    I crossed in a chugging mal-
combusting automobile
                    overland through Italy
with V., in love with her, in
                    love with the travel itself:
Croatia, Bosnia, coasts,

Kosovo, Montenegro,
Greece and on to Turkey. West-
ward again, to Venice and
through old Ottoman borders
to eat trout hooked in becks be-
yond smoky village inns, to
drink to strangers calm or loud,
to trace pilgrimage, pillage
or pleasure, to witness spies,
cries, clouds, crushed histories of
uprisings and colonies,
to seize on endless seasons
of blurred bullet holes in un-
repaired Madrid and Berlin,
the dark dry pocks of brute night
executions in stucco
whitewashed hamlets and roadside
walls of Andalucía,
high bridges to safety in
Switzerland that had been barred,
yet also, to see the wine-
celebrated survivals
by grace, luck, strength, and courage;
Cernuda, Lorca, Hikmet,
I read greedily, slowly
eyed Goya and Velázquez,
sought hoarse singing and guitars.
Later the return trip, by
ship again, through icebergs this
time to thick disorderly
democratic spruce, maple,
beech and birch forests of cold
northeastern America,
colossus, then all the way
back overland in the same
stuttering car again to
the Pacific, but in my

case *not* having invented

> a new way of writing, think-

ing or dreaming, in fact not

> able to grasp, although I

could sense it just beyond reach,

> a new understanding of

our time of beginnings, ends.

6.

[1972] In February in a small rented house standing alone amid grapefruit groves near the southeast coast of Spain, in the province of Murcia, V. and I stayed with friends for a week, listening at night to mice overhead in the ceiling playing soccer with a kernel of corn; we were talking, eating and drinking cheaply, we frugal rootless resting travelers not obligated to anyone or anything but ourselves for a brief while. Wild asparagus was ripe growing along low crude stone walls in terraced white-blossoming almond orchards; the countryside was patrolled by pairs of slow-witted Guardia Civil with alien patent-leather hats and ancient rifles—young recruits from orphanages in those last years of the dictatorship of Francisco Franco. One chilly afternoon, out behind the house a small flock of sheep arrived, and one shepherd, a man much older than I, holding a long stick. I had never labored in anything like that way. I assumed that I never would. I poured two small glasses full of Spanish brandy and I went out to meet him, carrying them before me in both hands. He was surprised, but in a formal, self-possessed way, as befitted converse with a stranger, a foreigner, he was friendly, he drank the brandy slowly holding each sip in his mouth to savor it fully and let it warm him. He had a small cloth bag of possessions and only a dozen or so sheep. As these grazed on the thin grass, one, a ram, he twice cracked casually but hard over the head with the long stick—for what offense I, knowing nothing of sheep, and only beginning to know something of Spain, could not guess. There was about him a kind of calm, an absence of striving, an unmistakable but to me nearly incomprehensible standing apart from the way I knew how to live, and from the way that the people I had met in Madrid lived, workers and shopkeepers in my neighborhood, and scholars, writers, the president of a foundation. There could be no hurry in this man's life; nor could I understand the extent, the unremittingness, of his solitude and exposure to life without a roof. On the low, flat-topped mountains nearby, there would be green summer grazing, toward which he was headed. He wore a dark cape over dark clothes; the nights were still cold. *"Ah señor,"* he said, *"No parece usted saber mucho de las dificultades de los pastores ahora. Las cosas han cambiado. Como es extranjero, usted no puede comprender que nuestro Señor viniera alguna vez a estos humildes pueblos . . ."* "Sir," he said, "you probably do not know much about the difficulties of shepherds these days. Things have changed. And being a foreigner, you can't understand that Our Lord came one time to these humble villages. Yes, it is true. Perhaps where you are from, there is very little sun, or none at all, since, even in summer, so many of you come here to stay in the sun all day at the shores of the sea, women scarcely wearing any clothing. But you are not aware, I believe, that more important than the sun are the footsteps of Our Lord. I have seen it myself, shown in a film, that he rode a donkey through my own village, only a few hours from here by foot." It was as he told me this, holding the glass of brandy on one hand, that twice with whip-quick motion of his stick in his other he rapped the head of the ram, making a sound as if he had struck a stone. He scarcely had looked at the beast; the beast scarcely reacted, and its uncanny unmammalian eyes in any case seemed indifferent, focused single-mindedly on something the shepherd and I could not see, and of far greater importance than we. "Do you travel always on foot?" I asked him. "Always when I am with my flock," he said. "But every year after shearing time I stay a while at my sister's house, and there I have a little motorbike." He smiled suddenly. "I call it Rocinante. Do you know the name?" We were standing behind the rented house, in a patch of open grass among the citrus groves in the thousand-year-old day that contained oranges, sadness, belief, nonbelief, stories. Another encounter had been offered to me that I had every reason on that day to accept, to live, and then try to imagine.

7.

My English mentor, dissent-   [1973–74]
           er still and anything but
a latter-day Romantic,
           with the drifting Navy Flake

smoke from his pipe would signal
                    me toward new directions
where Pound, Oppen, Tomlinson,
                    Bunting, but Hardy too, stood
along the lines like statues
                    thinking the verses I heard,
leading and eluding me.
                    In my tree-shaded student
mornings (my Russian tea, text,
                    notebook from Spain, my talis-
manic shard from a ploughed field
                    in Ionic Greece, Turkish
cigarettes), Roethke whispered
                    to the mud, Jeffers kept his
feelings clean, Du Fu recalled
                    despair of war and civil
service, Rich descended steps
                    against the Law, re-versed them,
Levertov breathlessly prayed
                    sensuous invitations,
whirling metaphors flew from
                    Ginsberg, at loud group meals my
young friends contested, laughed, raged
                    under home-made murals of
Inferno at New Pisa
                    in San Francisco and at
the Basque Hotel, where shepherds
                    down from the Sierra ate
sheepless in corners, and on
                    Saturday mornings Jaime
de Angulo's singsong strange
                    accent on radio re-
told of bird-people, roaring
                    monsters, delicate fates or
demonic ones, and our crowds
                    massed, chanted, threw stones to break
reactionary windows,

                    distant fires rose from forests
and air raids, from the unsafe
                    houses of home terrorists.
We thought; we could not fly, nor
                    would my shaking sense of things
resolve, my incurable
                    arrhythmia of feeling.

    8.

    my illustrations swallow up my thesis

    I feel too intensely the omnipresence of all in each, platonically
    speaking—or psychologically my brain fibres, or the spiritual Light
    which abides in the brain marrow as visible Light appears to do in
    sundry rotten mackerel & other <u>smashy</u> matters, is of too general an
    affinity with all things—and tho' it perceives the <u>difference</u> of things,
    yet is eternally pursuing the likenesses, or rather that which is
    common

    bring me two things that seem the very same, & then I am quick
    enough to shew the difference, even to hair-splitting—but to go on
    from circle to circle till I break against the shore of my Hearer's
    patience, or have my Concentricals dashed to nothing by a Snore—
    that is my ordinary mishap. At Malta, however, no one can charge
    me with one or the other. I have earned the general character of
    being a quiet well meaning man, rather dull indeed—& who would
    have thought, that he had been a <u>Poet</u>! 'O very wretched Poetaster,
    Ma'am! As to the reviews, it is well known, he half ruined himself
    in paying cleverer fellows than himself to write them' &c—25
    Dec[ember] 1804

He satirized himself, so;
                    he lamented—to the self
whom he revised by writing

                    his journals—his shattered in-
consolable grief over
                    his lost love, his wrong marriage,
and he chided himself for
                    failings—for example, his
sloth, or his "Mahometan
                    Superstition—dread as to
the destruction of Paper."
                    While secretary to the
Governor of Malta—his
                    perhaps cowardly attempt
to make an escape from his
                    marriage and a living, he
described this curious dread:

> I am almost ashamed to confess to myself, what pulling back of
> Heart I feel whenever I wish to light a candle or kindle a fire with
> a Hospital or Harbour Report and what a cumulus lie upon my
> Table, I am not able to conjecture what use they can ever be, and
> yet trembling lest what I thus destroyed might be of some use, in
> the way of knowle[d]ge. Thus seems the excess of a good feeling;
> but it is ridiculous. Monday Feb[ruary] 11, 1805.

His care for official writs—
                    however useless—seems to
show him at a moment when
                    he even identifies
himself with rule, with the state.

                    His endless thought and writing;
his crises endless, also.
                    His quondam hatred of hot
monarchical sugar-scum,
                    fear of the illiterates
he'd once defended . . . There'd be

no more strenuous pamphlets,
letters, clandestine fireside
hours while, cold and quaking, he
dried his sopping shoes, argued
that common people should be
freed from tyranny, hunger,
mistaken concepts, drink, jails,
that they should not be punished
for ignorance from which they
had had no means of escape.
What an eon had passed since
he had preached long last-minute
sermons stuffed with chapters and
verses to support his then
revolutionary Christ,
he could not let himself feel
anguish for the poor as they
desperately tried to cling to
slanted bowsprits of the king's
merchants, bankers, noblemen.

(And in my time, to those of
CEOs, celebrities,
flacks, flakes, pimps, war patriots?)

9.

Samuel Taylor Coleridge,
you ask at the edge of all
you have endeavored to think
through: "Those Whispers just as you
have fallen or are falling
asleep—what are they and whence?"   [4–8 March 1805]

The many that you saw in
                    one, the perhaps reconciled
opposites in their balance:
                    Oneness and Plurality,   [13–18 December 1803]
"endless Variety in
                    Identity," multitude   [19–21 October 1803]
and Unity, and your twice-   [13–15 December 1804]
                    recorded fantasy: "I
would make a pilgrimage to
                    the burning sands of Arab-
ia, or &c &
                    c[,] to find the Man
who could explain to me [how]
                    there can be <u>oneness,</u> there be-
ing infinite Perceptions."   [November 1799; October 1803]
                    Were irreconcilable
opposites what murmured in
                    the night?—voices of the too
many thoughts that came crowding
                    from within—the too many
English men and women whose
                    cries you could no longer bear?
So perhaps you displaced real
                    suffering and clamor of
the thick human crowd onto
                    the appealing green fronds that
need no literacy nor
                    franchise—this is the image
before your mind's eye—lovely
                    "Fern . . . scattered thick but growing
single"; and still they grow in
                    our unavoidable self-
conscious self-dividedness,
                    our heritages at odds,
our paper trails and trials of
                    spills and slips, they are growing
in our back seats and wet shoes,

in our mulch of paychecks, in
our notebooks red-inked from our
                        dialectical bloodstreams,
our wish to reconcile the
                        many and the one, power
and the governed, word and act.

10.

If I successfully tell
                        of a few of his and my
representative moments,
                        shot through with insoluble
political and also
                        poetic dilemmas, then
I have done nothing more than
                        compare myself to him with-
out justification; if
                        I confine to him what I
tell, I'm merely cutting and
                        pasting from detective work
done by someone else. If I
                        recount his decline and his
retreat from early powers,
                        words, sympathies, then what I
say may seem only bloodless,
                        and anyway will be far
from what poetry is now
                        like.

                        (*Fragmenting itself while*
murmuring at a full-length
                        mirror, or conditioning
its hair, or failing to raise

the heavy beams of as yet
uncreated consciousness,
                    or running the long lonely
distances, or making the
                    audience laugh, or leave, or
intimate, personal and
                    linguistically modest
to a fault, or by contrast,
                    surreal with lots of flash, gym-
nastic metaphorizing,
                    fast-paced non sequiturs, man-
nerisms, and, thrown in some-
                    times for the rhetorical
effect, what seems a casual
                    "spirituality"—un-
like the fervid expressions
                    of frightened faith in writings
by STC himself.) In
                    addition, there's the psycho-
logical dimension of
                    Coleridge's notebooks, and

anyone who does not re-
                    cognize the extent to which
early and intimate re-
                    lationships have given a
decisive shape to later
                    life is willfully seeking
to be emotionally
                    blind; or blinded—the lover
sleepwalks uncaressed, the child
                    cannot overcome her in-
visibility, a boy
                    beats another's face because
it's his father's . . . and what of
                    angry men voting for the

confident senator, sleek

as an otter, men who use

him to justify their knee-

kicks and their hungry pricks, their

crying need for enemies

and idols . . .—What? Can't I, too,

provide shots of new widows

and cute pets? Sexual sandal

scandals? A wide-screen itch to

bomb, a few brides upside down

in ditches? A bog-mummy

blog or a doggy bag? New

shampoos, or gold medals round

the crooked necks of loyal

consiglieri? And to

think that only a moment

ago we were in a poem!

11.

In order to evoke him-

self as he wished to be, he

had joined with Wordsworth to draw

into their poetry new

subjects from the common life,

from fantasy, reverie

and political ideals.

But the cabin boy in his

notebooks is perhaps the last

object he chose that belonged

to this earlier self he

was leaving behind him. Yet

he continued to ponder

how to understand spirit,

mind, being. He wrote: "all the

subtler parts of one's nature,

must be <u>solitary</u>—Man

                    exists herein to himself

& to God alone / —yea, in

                    how much only to God—how

much lies <u>below</u> his own"—he

                    uses this word—"Consciousness."   [October 1803]

Awareness. Or as image,

                    earlier: "A River, so

translucent as not to be

                    seen—and yet murmuring—shad-

owy world—& these a Dream /

                    Inchanted River." (And, if   [1802?]

our "nature" is just to be

                    solitary, and our thought

is as "natural" as a

                    river, then what's our social

obligation? I feel the

                    attraction of a psycho-

logical alibi for

                    not saving the cabin boy . . .)

Here's Coleridge's sense of

                    unconscious life, recorded

after evidently he

                    had taken a dose of drugs:

Wednesday—Afternoon. Abed—nervous—had noticed the prismatic
colours transmitted from the Tumbler—Wordsworth came—I talked
with him—he left me alone—I shut my eyes—beauteous spectra of
two colors, orange and violet—then of green, which immediately
changed to Peagreen, & then actually *grew* to my eye into a beauti-
ful moss, the same as is on the mantle-piece at Grasmere.—abstract
Ideas—& unconscious Links!!

                                                     [1801]

Does he already shift "un-

        conscious" from "latent ideas

in general" to "ideas

        keeping apart from conscious-

ness in spite of their inten-

        sity and activity"?

(Freud, 1912, *OED*)

        And now unconsciously I

choose him by intuition

        merely; yet also, I am

sure, in order to evoke

        in myself some aspect I

sense is either wanting or

        must be strengthened before I

can proceed any further.

        Or because I am frightened

and STC gives me his

        permission to retreat? Un-

deniable resemblance

        links his moment with my own,

though not poetically.

        Two second-hand volumes of

his notebooks I bought back then   [1973?]

        (1794 to

1804): I did not

        then understand how we use

what we read. I was drawn, in

        awe, to the many pages

of gladdening names of plants;

        especially wildflowers   [1800]

(written not in STC's

        hand but in that of his, so

he thought, real love, "Asra"). I

        grasped at Coleridge's pro-

fuse illustrations and could

     not comprehend his theses.
Of my time so much, as he
     of his (similar ages
of hope then horror, hope *and*
     horror), I went outside, where
some flower books grow, where thick
     ferns shake themselves in the wind.   [2004–07]

Notes

"At a twenty-four-hour gas station": *Todo es puerta—basta la leve presión de un pensamiento.* (Everything is a door—the light pressure of a thought is enough.)—Octavio Paz.

"In an old cabinet": *Oxford English Dictionary:*

> 1917 *Sun* (N.Y.) 5 Aug. III. 3/6 Variously spelled Jas, Jass, Jaz, Jazz, Jasz and Jascz. The word is African in origin. It is common on the Gold Coast of Africa and in the hinterland of Cape Coast Castle. Ibid. 3/7 Jazz is based on the savage musician's wonderful gift for progressive retarding and acceleration guided by his sense of 'swing.'

"Fern-Texts": Source texts are *Coleridge's Notebooks: A Selection,* edited by Seamus Perry (New York: Oxford University Press, 2002); *The Notebooks of Samuel Taylor Coleridge,* edited by Kathleen Coburn, vol. 1, *1794–1804* (Princeton, N.J.: Princeton University Press, 1957). Samuel Taylor Coleridge = 1772–1834. Coleridge's marriage to Sarah Fricker left him bitter and irresponsible; he believed, but perhaps unreasonably, that the love he then conceived for Sara Hutchinson ("Asra," in Coleridge's private name for her), the sister of Wordsworth's wife, Mary, would have been requited had he not already been married. William Wordsworth = 1770–1850.

Regarding Coleridge's sense of the unconscious, here are two entries from the *Oxford English Dictionary.* First, an idea; second, the earlier example from which perhaps the idea grew:

> 1817 COLERIDGE *Biographia Literaria, Poesy or Art,* In every work of art there is a reconcilement of the external with the internal; the conscious is so impressed on the unconscious as to appear in it.

> 1800 COLERIDGE *Christabel* II. xxvii, Still picturing that look askance With forced unconscious sympathy Full before her father's view.

After Freud, we also understand the relationship in the first quotation inversely, that in a work of art, the unconscious is so impressed upon the artist's (inevitably limited) conscious choices as to appear in them.

"My English mentor" = Donald Davie (1922–1995), author of *Articulate Energy: An Enquiry into the Syntax of English Poetry* (1955) and *Collected Poems* (1991).

Printed in the United States
132295LV00011B/5/P

9 780807 133187